"The invention and c... munications device, ... Caninebarkoencefflee- ohgraph,' by Dr. Victor D. Canineorkian, Phdog, is a truly remarkable achievement which has issued in a whole new era of communications between man and his best friend. For the first time in history, man and dogs can now talk to each other, and this powerful *Handbook* should make more of an impact on the future development of man and dogs than the discovery of fire and the invention of the wheel combined!

"I was deeply touched by many of the things that dogs told Dr. Canineorkian during his interviews with them which are in the *Handbook*. For example, these two DOGisms . . . *'Cats shouldn't have 8 more lives than dogs.'* . . . and . . . *'Water always tastes better out of a toilet!'*

"My higher consciousness to the wit and wisdom of dogs was also elevated to greater heights when I discovered in the *Handbook* that dogs can compose poetry (DOGoems). For example, this DOGoem . . . *'Roses are red, violets are blue, I hate cats, and if you like them, I hate you too!'*

"This book has had a profound effect on my own consciousness, for it has propelled me into an entirely new way of thinking and acting around dogs. When I look into the eyes of a dog now, I have the comforting thought of knowing that I can carry on a conversation with that dog using Dr. Canineorkian's new miraculous communications device!

"The *Handbook* has provided me with the motivation to pursue higher consciousness in my own books and tapes."

Dr. Helen Hound
Author:
Your Erroneous Chewstick
Pulling Your Own Tail
How to Be a No-Limit Dog
Life Is Empty Without Bones
Gifts from Your Master's Refrigerator
The "Walk-a-Mile for a Pig Ear" Diet

▲

Handbook to
HIGHER
CONSCIOUSNESS
to the
Wit and Wisdom
of Dogs

▲

Dr. Victor D. Canineorkian, Phdog

MOON RIVER
PUBLISHING
SAVANNAH
GEORGIA

A 🐾 BOOK

TRIBUTE TO A DOG

The one absolutely unselfish friend that man can have in this selfish world, the one that never deserts him, the one that never proves ungrateful or treacherous, is his dog. A man's dog stands by him in prosperity and in poverty, in health and in sickness. He will sleep on the cold ground where the wintry winds blow and the snow drives fiercely, if only he may be near his master's side. He will kiss the hand that has no food to offer; he will lick the wounds and sores that come in encounter with the roughness of the world. He guards the sleep of his pauper master as if he were a prince. When all other friends desert, he remains. When riches take wings and reputation falls to pieces, he is as constant in his love as the sun in its journey through the heavens.

GEORGE GRAHAM VEST

DEDICATION

*This book is dedicated
to all human beings, dogs,
and other animals on earth
who by living, loving
and laughing
can make our planet
a better place to live.*

CONTENTS

DOGisms (by subject)

DOGoems (by title)

Lorrie (L) and Holly Canineorkian

ACKNOWLEDGMENTS

The author is particularly appreciative of the part played by each of the dogs from all over the United States and Canada who allowed me to interview them. Each dog took time out from their busy schedule to talk with me and provided the DOGisms, DOGoems, and other wit and wisdom that made this book possible.

Also special thanks to my two Golden Retrievers, Holly and Lorrie, who have been my constant companions and who motivated me to develop the "Caninebarkoenceffleeohgraph" and to take on this book project.

During the development of the device, they never left my side and provided me with over 10,000 "test barks" and other dog sounds that were needed to fine tune it. They also played a vital role in each of the interviews and consulted with me on the final manuscript.

Dr. Victor D. Canineorkian, Phdog
Savannah, Georgia

FOREWORD

by **Walter Woofwoof, Editor**
Flea & Tick Quarterly

If you glanced across a campfire in the Stone Age some 14,000 years ago, you might have seen dogs that looked a lot like those in your neighborhood today. But, for the last 140 centuries, even though dogs and human beings have grown smarter and shared their food, dwellings and lives, they have still never been able to talk to each other.

All of that has now suddenly changed with the development of a miraculous new communications device by Dr. Victor D. Canineorkian, Phdog, a world-renowned Psycho-Canineologist. With this device, known as a "Caninebarkoenceffleeohgraph," man can now carry on a conversation with his best friend.

After developing the "Caninebarkoenceffleeohgraph," Dr. Canineorkian took it on the road and used it to interview hundreds of dogs all over the U.S. and Canada. The data he collected from his conversations with dogs enabled him to write this *Handbook* and answer many of the questions that man has had about dogs for thousands of years. Questions like: How do dogs feel about things they experience in their daily lives? What do they have on their minds during the day? What is really important to them? What would they like to say to their owners and to others if they could speak? Can dogs compose poetry?

Before reading this book, I urge you to see Appendix 1 and read the interview with Dr. Canineorkian by Barry Bones, editor of *The Backyard Journal*, a highly respected publication that stays on the "digging edge" of what's happening in back yards all over America! The interview explores Dr. Canine-orkian's professional credentials, how he developed the "Caninebarkoenceffleeohgraph," how the device works, and how he used it to gather the material to write this powerful *Handbook*.

After reading the *Handbook to Higher Consciousness to the Wit and Wisdom of Dogs*, I know that your world will never be the same again once you have viewed it through the eyes of a dog!

DOGisms

Book Order Form

Handbook to Higher Consciousness to the Wit and Wisdom of Dogs may be obtained through your local bookstore, or you may order it by sending a check or money order for $8.95 US / $11.95 CAN* plus $3.00 for shipping charges to:

Moon River Publishing
c/o Publication Services, Inc.
824 W. 10th, Suite 100
Austin, TX 78701

OR Call our toll-free number: 1-800-460-6690

Before you call, please fill out the order form below and have your credit card number and expiration date handy. Credit cards only—sorry, no C.O.D. orders.

OR Order by fax: 512-322-0694

Fax orders must be placed with a credit card only. Please sign this order form where indicated and enter your card number and expiration date. Georgia residents must add 6% sales tax.

I'd like to order ___ copies of *Handbook to Higher Consciousness*

to the Wit and Wisdom of Dogs at $8.95 each ($11.95 Canadian)*   _____

Postage and handling $3.00 per book   _____

Subtotal   _____

Georgia residents add 6% sales tax   _____

TOTAL ENCLOSED   _____

Ship to _____

Street _____ Apt./Suite# _____

City/State/Zip _____

Daytime Phone _____

Method of Payment

☐ **Check or Money Order** payable to *Moon River Publishing*

☐ **Credit card:** ☐ AMEX [AMERICAN EXPRESS]   ☐ MASTERCARD [MasterCard]   ☐ VISA [VISA]   ☐ DISCOVER [DISCOVER]

Credit Card No. _____

Expiration date___/___/___ Signature _____

* **Canadian orders:** We accept payment by cashier's check, money order or credit card only. No personal checks or C.O.D. shipments. Payment must be in U.S. funds.

Rolling on dead birds
makes the best perfume.

An ounce of chocolate
is worth a pound
of dog food.

Never leave home
without your bone.

Cats shouldn't have
8 more lives than dogs.

Food always tastes better
off the floor.

Happiness is a
bacon wrapped chewstick.

Life is empty
without a bone.

See and hear twice as much
as you bark.

Tennis balls are for mouths,
not rackets.

No one should have to go
through life
without sunglasses.

"Coming in season"
doesn't mean you're going
to Miami Beach.

Car windows are for sticking
your head out of.

Smoked pig ears are gifts
from God.

Never trust a cat.

When you age 7 times faster than people, you deserve more respect.

Fireplugs and mailboxes can be "draining."

Scratching and chewing
is good exercise.

Garbage men
make hair stand up
on your back.

You deserve to snore
with a nose full of dirt.

Mud puddles make
the best grooming parlors.

True love is a pizza with raw
hamburger topping.

Sleeping 20 hours a day
doesn't mean you're
brain dead.

Relief is spelled . . .
FIREPLUG!

I'd walk a mile for a pig ear.

Anyone who rolls on dead
birds is a friend of mine.

Be generous, give blood
to a tick and shelter to a flea.

Bark when you feel like it.

Consider who'll get your
bones when you die.

"Woofing" is the
art of swallowing
without tasting.

Shrimp breath is never
caused from eating shrimp.

Never criticize anyone
for chasing their tail.

Bones and bitches
are a winning combination.

Always have clear title
to your back yard.

Never trust your ball
to a stranger.

Always think through
your nose.

Give me meat or
give me candy.

A bitch in heat is music to the nose.

Always raise your tail in the company of strangers.

Never bite the hand
that "treats" you.

Sniffing beats kissing
any day.

Sofas are softer
than grass.

Never complain
if you eat something
different every day.

Bodies are retirement homes
for fleas.

If your water bowl stays
empty for 3 days, you've been
mistaken for a camel.

Barking keeps your throat
in shape.

Noses are for finding rotten
things to roll on.

Ice cream and cake
will give you wisdom.

A T-bone a day keeps
the Vet away.

Cars shouldn't be named
after cats.

Don't wait for your bone
to come in.
Go out and dig it up.

Butterfinger chewsticks
would change the world.

Spin around at least 3 times
before eating.

Garbage cans are made
to be turned over.

Never pass up a fireplug.

Smoked beef hooves
make you run faster.

Hide your bones
before leaving the yard.

Getting a driver's license
shouldn't be based on the
number of legs you have.

With Rollerblades,
we could conquer the world.

The 5 most important words
in any language —
The pizza man is coming!

Party food should always be
eaten before the guests
arrive.

Never roll on anything
that's not rotten.

Water always tastes better
out of a toilet.

A day without meat
is like a day
without sunshine.

Happiness is keeping your
nose in the dirt.

Never lie down
without scratching.

Never leave a "surprise"
on a front lawn without
someone watching.

What stays on the kitchen
counter is yours;
what hits the floor is mine!

Any pill you take
should be hidden inside of
a pound of peanut butter.

Chasing cars should be an
Olympic event.

A cheeseburger a day
keeps the Vet away.

"Make my day" — with
french fries and onion rings.

Mystery meat never makes
its own gravy.

Four legs are better
than two.

Real Bar-B-Que
is a smoked pig ear.

DOGoems

Book Order Form

Handbook to Higher Consciousness to the Wit and Wisdom of Dogs may be obtained through your local bookstore, or you may order it by sending a check or money order for $8.95 US / $11.95 CAN* plus $3.00 for shipping charges to:

Moon River Publishing
c/o Publication Services, Inc.
824 W. 10th, Suite 100
Austin, TX 78701

OR Call our toll-free number: 1-800-460-6690

Before you call, please fill out the order form below and have your credit card number and expiration date handy. Credit cards only—sorry, no C.O.D. orders.

OR Order by fax: 512-322-0694

Fax orders must be placed with a credit card only. Please sign this order form where indicated and enter your card number and expiration date. Georgia residents must add 6% sales tax.

I'd like to order ___ copies of *Handbook to Higher Consciousness*

to the Wit and Wisdom of Dogs at $8.95 each ($11.95 Canadian)*   _____

Postage and handling $3.00 per book   _____

Subtotal   _____

Georgia residents add 6% sales tax   _____

TOTAL ENCLOSED   _____

Ship to _____

Street _____

Street _____Apt./Suite# _____

Daytime Phone _____

Method of Payment

☐ **Check or Money Order** payable to *Moon River Publishing*

☐ **Credit card:** ☐ AMEX AMERICAN EXPRESS   ☐ MASTERCARD MasterCard   ☐ VISA VISA   ☐ DISCOVER DISCOVER

Credit Card No. _____

Expiration date____/____/____ Signature _____

* **Canadian orders:** We accept payment by cashier's check, money order or credit card only. No personal checks or C.O.D. shipments. Payment must be in U.S. funds.

CHASING CARS

The thrill of victory,
the agony of defeat,
chasing cars down the street.

My father before me,
my uncle and aunt,
they all chased cars
so don't tell me I can't.

You know,
it's really quite a thrill,
to miss a car
and take a spill.

So instead of wasting my time,
looking for some bitch in heat,
I'm chasing cars,
down the street!

FIREPLUGS

Oh, what a majestic sight,
standing so proud and tall,
with all of my favorite scents and smells,
sprayed upon its walls.

Many of my friends before me,
have made their presence known,
so now it's my turn,
to decorate this throne.

So I sniff and sniff,
and sniff and sniff,
and move around the base,
and something inside my bladder says,
make haste, make haste, make haste.

So I get into position,
and cock the old back leg,
and in the twinkle of an eye,
I've emptied out my keg.

And when I'm finally finished,
and the last drop hits the sand,
I know that everyone who passes this way,
will know that I'm a man!

PERFUMING THE BODY

Find a dead and rotten bird,
and roll from head to toe,
roll and roll, and roll and roll,
'til you can't roll no more.

Then take the smell with you,
and pass quickly through the door,
then look up at your master,
and roll all over the floor.

And when he screams and shouts,
and says you smell like hell,
just wag your tail and smile at him
and let him delight in your new smell.

This 'tis not shoddy,
'tis the best way to perfume the body!

BONES

Bones, bones, every where,
and all the yard did shrink,
bones, bones, everywhere,
it's hard for me to think.

Some bones are new,
and some are old,
but their taste and smell,
touches my very soul.

So when I die,
please bring me back,
as a clone,
of my favorite bone!

CATS

Roses are red,
violets are blue,
I hate cats,
and if you like them,
I hate you too!

COLLARS

They come in all sizes and colors,
some in red, white and blue,
but I've never found a collar yet,
that didn't choke you.

So why do I have to wear one,
when it's so tight around my neck,
and with all those stupid little tags,
I'm turning into a wreck.

Go ahead and pull it off of me,
and really set me free,
I promise I won't run away,
just try it and you'll see!

DIGGING

I dig all day in between meals,
and my backyard looks like a real mine field.

I never dig to bury a bone,
I dig cause I love it,
and it makes me feel like a King on his throne.

One of these days,
I'm going to get me a shirt,
with these 4 words on it,
"GOD, I LOVE DIRT!"

RIDING IN A CAR

When I'm out riding in a car,
I feel like a movie star,
with my head out the window,
taking in every sight,
and my ears catching the wind,
and flying like a kite.

I smile at a few drivers,
and bark at all the rest,
but to just go out cruising around,
is what I love to do best!

NOSES

It isn't very hard to see,
what my nose does for me.

It can root around in the dirt,
or smell out a dirty sock or shirt.

It can pick up the scent of a garbage can,
or find something rotten to roll on in the sand.

It can smell out a piece of raw meat,
or a cookie, biscuit, or doggie treat.

It can smell a dozen quail,
or detect a mailman bringing the mail.

It can smell chocolate or anything sweet,
or find a bitch that's gone in heat.

It can smell out things smaller than a mouse,
or detect a burglar entering a house.

It can smell a kitchen full of bugs,
or a box of cocaine and other drugs.

So now I hope that you can see,
what my nose does for me!

GARBAGE CANS

I like to run around,
and kick up some sand,
but what really turns me on,
is knocking over a garbage can.

Sometimes I even get lucky,
and find a little meat,
that's an added bonus,
and a very special treat!

CHEW STICKS

You must be sick,
to give me a chewstick,
What I need at my age,
is something easy to chew,
like a pound of prime sirloin,
or a nice T-bone will do!

CHASING YOUR TAIL

There's no better sport around,
than chasing after your tail,
you run around in circles,
and wail, and wail, and wail.

You know you'll never catch it,
but it's still a lot of fun to try,
especially when it itches so bad,
that you think you're gonna die.

So when I'm old and gray,
and skinny, sick and frail,
I hope I can still run around in circles,
and chase after my tail!

FIGHTING MACHINE

Some say I'm not very nice,
others say I'm mean,
but I'm mighty proud that I was bred,
to be a fighting machine.

I've never tried to hide the facts,
or shed a lot of tears,
and I'm always the first one to admit,
that I've chewed a lot of ears.

So please don't judge me harshly,
Why not give me a break,
at least you always know where I stand,
because I sure ain't no fake!

DOG FOOD

Come here boy,
you always say,
I've got you a special treat,
but when I rush up to my bowl,
it's the same old mystery meat.

I try to act excited,
but it's getting harder for me to fake,
especially when I see you stuffing down,
a giant sirloin steak.

You know I'm not an average dog,
and I don't like my food served cold,
I'm your best friend and companion,
and I really do have a heart and a soul.

So if you want to make me happy,
and keep me in a good mood,
then throw away all of those cans and bags,
and start feeding me your food!

FLYING

I always start to crying,
when I know that I'll be flying.
You put me in a little box,
and shove me down below,
and before I can even look around,
they've slammed the cargo door,
and there ain't no light in there no more.

I'd much prefer to stay at home,
and be with all my mates,
instead of being crammed inside a plane,
with the baggage and the crates.

So the next time I go flying,
you'll be doing all the crying,
because instead of me being down below,
with the baggage and the mail,
I'll be in your First Class seat,
drinking a big cocktail!

DUCK HUNTING

I'm a lot older now,
and really start to tire,
so why can't I stay home,
and sleep by the fire.

I've never enjoyed breaking ice,
and freezing at the crack of dawn,
I'd much prefer to stay at home,
and chew on my favorite bone.

Go get'um boy, I always hear,
but why should I really care,
I'm not the only one who can float,
why don't you ever jump out of the boat,

So let me hang around the house,
and not go hunting anymore,
I don't even have web feet,
and I sure ain't no Labrador.

Maybe one day,
with a little luck,
I won't have to get up early,
and go chase after a stupid duck!

Appendices

Interview with
Dr. Victor D. Canineorkian, Phdog
by Barry Bones, Editor
The Backyard Journal

Barry Bones is editor of a highly respected trade publication, **The Backyard Journal**, *which stays on the "digging edge" of what dogs are doing in back yards all over America.*

This interview with world-renowned PsychoCanineologist Dr. Victor D. Canineorkian, Phdog, took place in a back yard in Virginia where Dr. Canineorkian had gone to interview a Basset Hound using his amazing "Caninebarkoenceffleeohgraph." This is a transcript of the interview by Mr. Bones.

BARRY BONES: Dr. Canineorkian, thank you so much for taking time out from your busy schedule to speak with me. Tell me something about your educational background and professional credentials.

DR. CANINEORKIAN: Certainly, Barry, but before I do, let me say that I feel you have a top-notch publication and I am especially impressed with your technical knowledge of backyards and your in-depth reporting. For example, the recent cover story you wrote on *"The Best Depth to Bury Bones to Maintain Maximum Flavor"*!

Now, concerning my educational background,. I'm a graduate of Chewstick University in Pigear, Oklahoma, with a BSniff Degree in PsychoCanineology. I also have a Phdog Degree with a special *"Flea/Tick Cluster"* from The Howling Institute in Wailing, Vermont.

BARRY BONES: I understand you are the only PsychoCanineologist on this planet who has this *"Flea/Tick Cluster"* recognition. What is it?

DR. CANINEORKIAN: Before I tell you about the special *"Flea-Tick Cluster"* recognition that I received with my doctorate degree, I'll tell you more about my background.

When I was eight years old, I woke up one morning and found that I had more fleas and ticks on my body than my old dog, *Itch.* This discovery, and major itch I might add, played a major role in "sending me to the dogs" at an early age, fueling my passion to conduct major flea/tick studies, and motivating me to develop a device that would enable me to talk to dogs to help me in my studies.

By the time I was 20 years old, I had read every trade journal on fleas and ticks that was available and was recognized as an expert in the field by PsychoCanineologists around the world. And, it was because of my great knowledge and expertise in this area that the board of trustees of The Howling Institute gave me the special *"Flea/Tick Cluster"* recognition. I'm very proud of this honor and having this recognition has helped me get funding for major dog research projects. It has also opened many kennel doors for me!

BARRY BONES: Tell me more about your major dog research projects.

DR. CANINEORKIAN: When I was 21 years old, I did my first major flea/tick study after receiving a $22 million grant from the U.S. Government to find out what was causing *"The Fleaing and Ticking of America."* This grant really catapulted my career, but it also put enormous pressure on me. I was told by many top bureaucrats in Washington, DC, including some in the White House, that I had to report my flea/tick findings within six months, or forfeit the $22 million!

BARRY BONES: Were you able to finish the study on time?

DR. CANINEORKIAN: Yes! I immediately went out and borrowed 357 dogs that were covered with fleas and ticks and set up a lab in my garage. It was a very tight space to have all those dogs and the smell began to get to me, but I was able to finish the study on time. In fact, I reported my findings in only five months, and sent a refund check back to the U.S. Government for $27.68 after receiving the $22 million!

BARRY BONES: What did you find out and report?

DR. CANINEORKIAN: After collecting over 37,000 pages of "doggie itch/scratch data," I concluded that 99.999% of male dogs and 98.666% of female dogs, of all breeds, sizes, and geographic locations, preferred to scratch their fleas rather than chase them all over their bodies and bite them! This was a significant finding, and I received a personal phone call from the President of the United States congratulating me for my work!

BARRY BONES: That's really impressive, doctor! I know how proud you must have been when you got a phone call from the President of the United States!

DR. CANINEORKIAN: Yes, that phone call and recognition by the President really put me on the map in Washington! In 1990 I received a six-year, $200 million grant from the U.S. Government to develop a device that would enable people to carry on conversations with dogs! It was a top secret project which was code named "Operation Bark-Bark." I began working on the device in a secret lab that was buried deep inside of a garbage dump in Chicago, Illinois.

BARRY BONES: Were you able to develop this device in six years as stipulated in the $200 million grant?

DR. CANINEORKIAN: Yes, and I only spent $199.999 million on its development and refunded the balance back to Washington! I called the device I developed a "Caninebarko-enceffleeohgraph."

BARRY BONES: Tell me more about your "Caninebarkoenceffleeohgraph" which many scientists and journalists around the world are saying is the greatest achievement in communications since cavemen stopped throwing rocks at each other and started talking!

DR. CANINEORKIAN: This is not a fly-by-night product that was developed to be sold on Cable TV for three easy payments of $19.95 each, plus shipping and handling charges. The development of this device was given the highest priority and top secret clearance by the U.S. Government. In fact, many members of Congress told me that it was vital to the security of the United States, and that we must have this device operational before any other country in the world, especially Iraq!

I was also told that this device would lead to the creation of a new government agency, *The Department of Canine Affairs*, which would oversee all "dog rights" in this country, from the development of dog food to the flavoring of chewsticks and pig ears! This agency would be headed by a "Top Dog" who would use the "Caninebarkoenceffleeohgraph" to report directly to the President of the United States!

BARRY BONES: Did government officials mention other uses to you for this device?

DR. CANINEORKIAN: Yes, some felt that it could be used to put "real dogs" on Capital Hill, maybe even have a Bulldog become Speaker of the House!

BARRY BONES: That's incredible! No wonder the project to develop this device was top secret. Tell me more about its development?

DR. CANINEORKIAN: As I mentioned before, it took me six years to develop the "Caninebarkoenceffleeohgraph." All of the development was done in a secret lab that was buried deep inside a garbage dump in Chicago, Illinois. No one in the area of the garbage dump ever knew what was really going on there, although some of the residents wondered why so much dog food was delivered to the dump each day!

BARRY BONES: How many dogs did you use to develop the device?

DR. CANINEORKIAN: At one point, I had over 600 dogs in the lab with me, but the smell was even starting to get to me so I cut it back to 308 dogs! I used tons of dog food during the development, and generated over 88,000 *dogabytes* of barking, wailing, howling, scratching, and sniffing data!

Holly and Lorrie, my two Golden Retrievers, were instrumental in the development of the "Caninebarkoenceffleeohgraph." They provided me with over 10,000 "test barks" and other dog sounds that were needed to fine tune it.

BARRY BONES: How does the instrument operate?

DR. CANINEORKIAN: It's really quite simple to operate even though top secret computer hardware and software are used inside the device. One set of headphones is placed on top of a dog's head and the other set is worn by the person who will be talking to the dog. The headphones are then connected to a "black box" which contains the "Bark-O-Implosion-Excellerator." This is the heart of the "Caninebarkoenceffleeohgraph" and where all of the sound and language conversions are translated and converted for the dog and the person to understand.

BARRY BONES: So, what you are really saying is that this device makes it possible for a dog and a person to carry on a two-way conversation. The dog can talk to the person and the person can talk to the dog. Is that correct?

DR. CANINEORKIAN: Yes, that's right. I felt that I had to have a two-way conversation. The device is designed so that a person's voice is quickly converted into dog barks and other dog sounds that the dog wearing the headphones can understand. It also quickly translates dog barks and other dog sounds into language that the person wearing the other set of headphones can understand.

BARRY BONES: So it's the "Bark-O-Implosion-Excellerator" that handles all of the voice conversions and translations?

DR. CANINEORKIAN: Yes, when the person talks to the dog, the "Bark-O-Implosion-Excellerator" quickly converts their voice into dog barks and other dog sounds so the dog can understand. And, when the dog speaks back to the person, his or her barks, growls and other dog sounds are quickly converted and translated inside the "Bark-O-Implosion-Excellerator" so that the person can understand what the dog is saying. I also installed a dial on the "black box" so that a southern and northern dialect can be fine tuned. I'm currently working on a "Redneck" tuner so dogs can better understand Rednecks!

BARRY BONES: Doctor, your device is truly amazing and will open up so many doors in the future. I'd like to borrow it the next time I do a cover story for *The Backyard Journal*!

What impact on man's and dogs' future development do you feel this communications device will have?

DR. CANINEORKIAN: I'm not sure what impact it will have on man/dog development in the future, but I do know that I could not have written the *Handbook* and answered many of the questions that man has had about dogs for thousands of years without using the "Caninebarkoenceffleeohgraph" to conduct my interviews with dogs all across America and Canada!

BARRY BONES: What is the name of your handbook, and how can people get a copy of it?

DR. CANINEORKIAN: My book is titled *Handbook to Higher Consciousness to the Wit and Wisdom of Dogs*, and may be obtained through a local bookstore, or someone can order it from the publisher by sending a check or money order for $8.95 U.S./$11.95 Canada, plus $3.00 for shipping charges to: Moon River Publishing, c/o Publication Services, Inc., 824 W. 10th, Suite 100, Austin, TX 78701. Or, they can order it by calling toll-free 1-800-460-6690 and charge it to American Express, MasterCard, Visa, or Discover.

BARRY BONES: Thank you, Dr. Canineorkian, for spending time with me today. One final question before you go. Are you currently working on any other top secret dog research projects?

DR. CANINEORKIAN: Yes, Barry, I am, but I can't discuss them with you now because they are top secret. However, I can tell you that you shouldn't be surprised if you see some "real dogs" on Capitol Hill in Washington in the near future!

Major Study of "Dogisms"

After developing the "Caninebarkoenceffleeohgraph," Dr. Canineorkian took it on the road, and used it to interview hundreds of dogs all across the U.S. and Canada. The data he collected resulted in the "DOGisms," "DOGoems" and other material that are in this powerful Handbook.

However, in his quest for the truth, Dr. Canineorkian wanted to verify that the "DOGisms" he was given by dogs during the interviews were true and not just made up! To verify their truth, he decided to pick three (3) of them and study them in depth. If he found those three (3) to be true, he could conclude that all of the other DOGisms he was given were true.

To conduct this study, Dr. Canineorkian received a $45 million U.S. Government Grant (*$15 million for each DOGism to be studied*). The study was completed in only three months and a refund check for $12.37 was returned to the U.S. Government for money he didn't spend.

The results of Dr. Canineorkian's in depth study of the three (3) "DOGisms" are given in A, B, and C below.

A. TRUE OR FALSE
DOGism:*"Rolling on dead birds makes the best perfume."*

To gather the data he would need to verify the truth of this DOGism, Dr. Canineorkian borrowed seven (7) dogs from the streets of Chicago, Illinois. He then set up the criteria for the selection of three (3) dead and rotten birds that he would use for the dogs to roll on.

The breed of bird was not relevant to the selection. What was relevant was the dead bird's "smell level" and geographic location!

Dr. Canineorkian then boarded the private jet he had purchased for the studies and went in search of the dead birds.

The first "very deceased" bird that he selected was found on the 8th hole of a major golf resort in Florida. The second dead bird was found near the 17th hole of a major golf resort in the Bahamas, and the last dead bird was found in a sand trap near the 13th hole at a golf resort in Bermuda.

When he got the dead birds back to the lab, he carefully recorded each bird's "smell level" on a *"Rot-o-grosstometer."* A normal dead bird should register in the range of 970 "smell-o-rots" on the *"Rot-o-grosstometer."* However, to his amazement, each bird he had selected registered over 1900. This meant that even he could only stay in the special "bird rolling chamber" for three minutes at a time, and would have to wear a face mask and breathing apparatus to keep from passing out!

After three days of extensive rolling tests, the seven (7) dogs loved their smell so much that they had to be physically removed from the chamber. Dr. Canineorkian then interviewed each dog and concluded that this "DOGism" . . . *Rolling on dead birds makes the best perfume* . . . was 100% true!

B. TRUE OR FALSE
DOGism: *"Tennis balls are for mouths, not rackets."*

To gather the data he would need to verify the truth of this "DOGism," Dr. Canineorkian borrowed three (3) Labrador Retrievers, three (3) Golden Retrievers, six (6) tennis balls, and six (6) tennis rackets.

After throwing the tennis balls and tennis rackets all over the lab for three days for the dogs to retrieve, all six (6) dogs only retrieved the tennis balls, not the rackets.

Dr. Canineorkian then interviewed each dog and quickly concluded that this "DOGism" . . . *Tennis balls are for mouths, not rackets* . . . was also 100% true!

C. TRUE OR FALSE
DOGism: *"I'd walk a mile for a pig ear."*

To gather the data he needed to verify the truth of this "DOGism," Dr. Canineorkian borrowed a very fat Dachshund and a rather chubby Basset Hound. He used these dogs for his experiment because he knew that walking a mile would require much more effort on their part with their short legs and stomachs dragging the ground, and this would offer even more conclusive proof of the results!

For the experiment, he needed two (2) pig ears and a one-mile stretch of deserted dirt road for the dogs to walk down.

Since this major study was funded by the U.S. Government, the cost of each pig ear was $2,500, and the cost to rent a one-mile stretch of dirt road from a farmer was $2.5 million!

A start/finish line was marked in the sand a mile apart, and a special device was attached to each dog's neck. The device held the pig ear and let it dangle back and forth just out of reach of the dog's mouth.

After four hours of walking and dragging their stomachs, the Dachshund crossed the finish line first, followed by the Basset Hound thirty minutes later.

Dr. Canineorkian then interviewed each dog and quickly concluded that this "DOGism" . . . *I'd walk a mile for a pig ear* . . . was also 100% true!

He then concluded that all of the DOGisms in this *Handbook* are true!

Note: If you would like to correspond with Dr. Victor D. Canineorkian, Phdog, write to:

Dr. Victor D. Canineorkian, Phdog,
Moon River Publishing,
c/o Publication Services, Inc.
824 W. 10th, Suite 100
Austin, TX 78701.

"People" Quotes About Dogs

The more I see of the
representatives of the people,
the more I admire my dogs.
ALPHONSE DE LAMARTINE

·:·

I think I have a right to resent,
to object to libelous statements
about my dog.
FRANKLIN DELANO ROOSEVELT

·:·

The world is going to the dogs.
THEODORA DUBOIS

·:·

A door is what a dog is perpetually
on the wrong side of.
OGDEN NASH

·:·

Let dogs delight to bark and bite,
For God hath made them so.
ISSAC WATTS

Recollect that Almighty,
who gave the dog to be a companion
of our pleasures and our toils,
hath invested him with a nature
noble and incapable of deceit.
SIR WALTER SCOTT

If you pick up a starving dog
and make him prosperous, he will not
bite you. This is the principal difference
between a dog and a man.
MARK TWAIN

The more I see of men,
the better I like my dog.
FREDERICK THE GREAT

If a dog's prayers were answered,
bones would rain from the sky.
PROVERB

A good dog deserves a good bone.
BEN JOHNSON, 1635

'Tis sweet to hear the watch-dog's honest bark
bay deep-mouth'd welcome as we draw near home;
'tis sweet to know there is an eye will mark
our coming, and look brighter when we come.
LORD BYRON

❧

The great pleasure of a dog is that you may
make a fool of yourself with him and not only
will he not scold you, but he will make
a fool of himself too.
SAMUEL BUTLER

❧

No one appreciates the very special genius of
your conversation as a dog does.
CHRISTOPHER MORLEY

❧

The best thing about a man is his dog.
FRENCH PROVERB

Dog with the pensive hazel eyes,
shaggy coat, or feet of tan,
what do you think when you look so wise
into the face of your fellow, man?
W.C. OLMSTED

Ask Holly Canineorkian

Dogs vs. Wives

DEAR HOLLY: Your columns have touched my life in so many ways and I bless you for the days you've brightened and the things you've taught me. You are part of our national heritage, and no day is complete until I read your column. Now would you please rerun my favorite column in which you showed the advantages of having a dog instead of a wife. I found a copy of it stuffed under the front seat of my wife's car, and this gem deserves to be repeated. Thanks a million from a devoted reader.

DEAR DEVOTED READER: Here it is with my pleasure. DOGS VS. WIVES . . . . We age seven times faster so you can trade

Continued on next page

us in on a new model more often . . . We will always lick your hand and love you no matter what sort of company you've been keeping . . . We will never need expensive dental work. Just give us a chewstick once in a while to keep our teeth clean and bright . . . We will never go out and buy expensive perfume. Just let us roll over a very deceased and rotten bird when we find one . . . We will never need to be told everyday that you love us. Just give us a slice of pizza and let more of your food hit the floor . . . We will never need to go to a beauty parlor to get our hair washed and cut. Just let us use a mud puddle in the back yard, and use the kitchen scissors to cut us . . . You'll never have to take us to an expensive restaurant. You can feed us the same food every day . . . We will never go on a diet and starve you to death . . . We never need clothes or shoes . . . We don't care what kind of car you drive. Just let us stick our head out the window . . . We will never divorce you and try to take you to the cleaners . . . We will never use your credit cards . . . We will never care how many football games you watch or how many beers you drink . . . You will never have to take us on an expensive cruise to some exotic place. Just take us swimming or hunting . . . And, finally, you will never have to buy us a new car or a mink coat. Just give us a few tennis balls to play with!

Ask Holly Canineorkian

Sounds Like "Fake Fat" to Me!

DEAR HOLLY: I went to a fast food restaurant the other day, and they said they were cooking the french fries in some substance that is slippery and passes right through your body without hanging around to clog your arteries and get you fat! I know how much you like french fries, and I'd like your comments on anything that you've heard about this stuff. Thanks a lot from a french fry freak!

DEAR FRENCH FRY FREAK: There is a food product that can be used to cook french fries and other foods that sounds to good to be true to me. I won't mention its

Continued
on next page

name because I don't want to have a dog house full of lawyers. I'll just refer to it as the "Big O"!

The "Big O" has been approved by your Food and Drug Administration (FDA), and I read that this stuff is a synthetic chemical that is made out of sugar and vegetable oil, and looks like regular fat but its molecules are too large and tightly packed to digest so it passes quickly through the body without stopping to clog arteries or fatten hips. It must be real slippery like your Teflon. Whatever it is, people sure don't need any more synthetic chemicals in their food, and I don't like it because I eat a lot of people food that is dropped on the floor.

If you don't believe me about too many synthetic chemicals in your food, listen to this. The other day I was cruising around the kitchen looking for anything that had fallen off the counter and hit the floor, and I found an empty soup can. Before I could stick my tongue inside the can to clean it out, I eye-balled the ingredients on the label, and I couldn't believe what I read was in that soup! The stuff sounded like rocket fuel to me . . . Ferrous Sulfate, Thiamine Mononitrate, Potassium Lactate, Disodium Inosinate, Disodium Guanylate . . . and who knows what else was in there! How can stuff like that be good for your body. No wonder there are so many sick people in this country!

Then there are the side effects from using the "Big O"! I heard it can act like a laxative and cause diarrhea, cramps, and

Continued
on next page

other gastrointestinal disturbances. I wonder how many fast food establishments that use it will install "Porta Potties" in their parking lots for customers who have eaten a large order of french fries and can't make it home in time! Also, can't you see someone rushing into a hospital emergency room in the middle of the night thinking they have an appendicitis only to find out a few hours later, and a few thousand dollars poorer, that the real culprit was the "Big O"!

I've also heard that the "Big O" can rob people of vitamins A, D, E and K. If that's true, that's like eating and starving yourself to death at the same time!

But, there is some light at the end of the tunnel. Your FDA will require that all products that use the "Big O" have a label warning of its side effects. That should do a lot of good! How many people do you know who smoke or drink and read the warning label on a pack of cigarettes or a can of beer?

All I can say to you and other people is good luck and happy eating, but please don't ever put that stuff in my dog food. I love "real fat" and need it in my diet!

What Dogs Tell Their Owners

In his interviews, Dr. Canineorkian asked some of the dogs what they would like to tell their owners. Here are their anonymous answers.

FEEDING ME: Why don't you try feeding me at the same time each day. Sometimes I feel like I live in 12 different time zones when it comes to your feeding me. I get so hungry that I bite off all of my nails, and then swallow two pounds of your linoleum kitchen floor! If you're not going to feed me for a few days, the least you could do is drop more of your food on the floor instead of into that fat mouth of yours!

GIVING ME A PILL: The next time you try to force a pill down my throat, if you haven't coated it with at least a pound of peanut butter, or hidden it inside of an ice cream sandwich, I'm going to take your arm off at the elbow!

GROOMING MYSELF: Stop yelling at me when I chew my nails, and lick and scratch myself at 3 o'clock in the morning. With you and the kids bugging me to death all the time, that's the only time I can groom myself! Also, stop telling me how bad I smell. If you were as tall as the exhaust pipe on your car, and your stomach dragged the ground, you would have a hard time staying clean yourself!

WASHING: I'd rather make friends with a Cat than be washed, flipped and dipped! Whatever they use to kill my fleas almost kills me! That's why I always go looking for something rotten to roll on the minute I get back home. If you would start giving me a bath in your bathtub, I promise I'll never roll on top of anything dead and rotten for at least a week, and I'll stay off of the sofa while you're watching the tube!

CLIPPING MY NAILS: Stop using your nail clippers to clip my nails. Spend a few bucks and get dog nail clippers, and make sure you don't cut my nails too short and make them bleed. If you make them bleed one more time, I'm going to make the house look like the return of the vampire, and I'm going to leave surprises everywhere!

BAD BREATH: Stop telling me that I've got shrimp breath and taking me to the vet to find out what's wrong with me. When you get up in the morning, your breath isn't exactly a bright ray of sunshine! You know perfectly well that I've always had shrimp breath, and I'm real proud of it. I'm also proud of my green teeth. Also, what do you expect my breath to smell like when you keep dropping pieces of candy bars on the floor for me to vacuum up!

LOW ENERGY: When I'm lying on my back in the living room catching a few rays of sunshine, stop accusing me of having low energy and then rushing me to the vet to find out what's wrong. He always tells you that I have low blood sugar and then tries to sell you a bunch of pills for me to take. Save your money! What I really need for more energy are candy bars at least 6 times a day. Any brand will do! You might also look into getting me a supply of butterfinger or peanut butter flavored chewsticks!

FLEAS: Fleas, like your taxes, are a real pain in the rear end. So, the next time I wake up in the middle of the night and start scratching and chewing on them, don't get so bitched off at me! You'd scratch and lick your own private parts if you had those small, reddish, flat little b——s all over you! If you want to sleep through the night, break down and give me a bath once or twice a year!

DOCKING AND CROPPING: If you ever try to cut and reshape my ears or shorten my tail, I'll bark at you at 3 o'clock every morning. I'll also make sure that I always sleep next to your bed when I have bad gas! How would you like it if someone docked and cropped you? Think what your friends would say about you!

DIET: An adequate diet is one that will maintain good health without the development of deficiency diseases. Remember that, dummy, the next time you try to feed me mystery meat or some of that cheap dog food that has no meat in it. Why can't you get it through that thick head of yours that what I really need is a nice warm meal every once in a while. I could also use some variety in my diet, like a T-bone steak with french fries! Stop believing that dogs are accommodating animals and will eat what you give them. That might have been true until you tossed half of your cheeseburger in the back seat of the car one day and I got a chance to taste what you've been eating!

Book Order Form

Handbook to Higher Consciousness to the Wit and Wisdom of Dogs may be obtained through your local bookstore, or you may order it by sending a check or money order for $8.95 US / $11.95 CAN* plus $3.00 for shipping charges to:

Moon River Publishing
c/o Publication Services, Inc.
824 W. 10th, Suite 100
Austin, TX 78701

OR Call our toll-free number: 1-800-460-6690

Before you call, please fill out the order form below and have your credit card number and expiration date handy. Credit cards only—sorry, no C.O.D. orders.

OR Order by fax: 512-322-0694

Fax orders must be placed with a credit card only. Please sign this order form where indicated and enter your card number and expiration date. Georgia residents must add 6% sales tax.

I'd like to order ___ copies of *Handbook to Higher Consciousness*

to the Wit and Wisdom of Dogs at $8.95 each ($11.95 Canadian)* _____

Postage and handling $3.00 per book _____

Subtotal _____

Georgia residents add 6% sales tax _____

TOTAL ENCLOSED _____

Ship to _____

Street _____Apt./Suite# _____

City/State/Zip _____

Daytime Phone _____

Method of Payment

☐ **Check or Money Order** payable to *Moon River Publishing*

☐ **Credit card:** ☐ AMEX **AMERICAN EXPRESS** ☐ MASTERCARD **MasterCard** ☐ VISA **VISA** ☐ DISCOVER **DISCOVER**

Credit Card No. _____

Expiration date____/____/____ Signature _____

* **Canadian orders:** We accept payment by cashier's check, money order or credit card only. No personal checks or C.O.D. shipments. Payment must be in U.S. funds.